Henry Newell

Plain talks on avoided subjects

Henry Newell

Plain talks on avoided subjects

ISBN/EAN: 9783742816054

Manufactured in Europe, USA, Canada, Australia, Japa

Cover: Foto ©Thomas Meinert / pixelio.de

Manufactured and distributed by brebook publishing software
(www.brebook.com)

Henry Newell

Plain talks on avoided subjects

PLAIN TALKS

ON

AVOIDED SUBJECTS.

HENRY N. GUERNSEY, M.D.

ON

AVOIDED SUBJECTS.

BY

HENRY N. GUERNSEY, M. D.,

*Ex-Professor of Obstetrics and Diseases of Women and Children in the
Homœopathic Medical College of Penn'a; Ex-Professor of Materia
Medica and Institutes in the Hahnemann Medical College
of Philadelphia and Dean of the Faculty; Author of
Guernsey's Obstetrics, including the Disorders
peculiar to Women and Young Children;
Lectures on Materia Medica, &c.*

*Honorary Member of the Hahnemannian Medical Institute of Phila-
delphia; of the Homœopathic Medical Society of the State of New
York; of the Instituto Homeopatico Mexicano; of the Hahnemannian Society of Madris de Tulio, Spain; Member of
the American Institute of Homœopathy; Consulting
Physician to the West Philadelphia Homœopathic Hospital for Children, &c. &c.*

PHILADELPHIA, PENN'A:

F. A. DAVIS, ATT'Y, PUBLISHER,

1882.

THIS LITTLE VOLUME IS FERVENTLY AND SOLEMNLY DEDICATED TO ITS MISSION.

THOSE WHO CONSCIENTIOUSLY READ AND FAITHFULLY APPLY ITS TEACHINGS TO LIFE, CANNOT FAIL TO BECOME WISER, BETTER AND HAPPIER MEMBERS OF THE HOME CIRCLE AND OF SOCIETY AT LARGE.

PREFACE.

FOR many years I have wished that some able pen would place before the community at large the knowledge contained in the following pages. Some of this information has appeared from time to time in such books as "Graham's Lectures on Chastity," "Todd's Students' Manual," and a few popular works of a similar kind, which have been of immense service to the human race in preserving chastity and in reclaiming the unchaste. But all these are now inadequate to the growing demand for more light on these vital topics. It has been too much the custom for everyone, parents included, to shrink from instructing their own children, or those entrusted to their care, on these points; consequently, many young people *solely from their ignorance* fall into the direst evils of a sexual nature and are thereby much injured and sometimes wholly ruined for life's important duties.

An experience of forty years in my professional career has afforded me thousands of opportunities for sympathizing with young men, and young women too, who had unconsciously sunk into these very evils merely for want of an able writer to place this whole subject truthfully and squarely before them, or for some wise friend to perform the same kind office verbally. The perusal of a work by

Wm. Acton, M. R. C. S., of London, on "The Functions and Disorders of the Reproductive Organs in Childhood, Youth, Adult Age, and Advanced Life," has, by his purity of sentiments, which have ever been identical with my own, both inspired and emboldened me to write a work of similar import. But his is for the profession while mine is for the profession and the laity, of both sexes and of any age. May its perusal inspire the readers with a higher appreciation of the matters herein treated, and with a greater effort to reformatory measures everywhere. Whenever I advise the consulting of a "judicious" (a term I use many times) physician, I mean one fully and practically qualified, both by inherent qualities and education for the fullest confidence of his patients.

I am indebted to my son, Joseph C. Guernsey, M. D., for assistance in editing and carrying this work through the press.

HENRY N. GUERNSEY, M.D.,

1423 Chestnut St., Philad'a.

JUNE, 1882.

CONTENTS.

CHAPTER I.

IN the creation of the world and all that therein is, we should consider it an axiom that "Everything was created for use." All individual substances, or beings, that come to our notice bear certain relations to one another, have connection one with another, and are dependent upon and useful to each other; and nothing could possibly exist or subsist without this co-relation: connection with and use to each other. This is a law which needs only a little reflection to be accepted as a truth in every particular—in the greatest as well as in the least created form. This is more plainly seen in the animal kingdom than in the mineral or vegetable, because its members associate and finally become conjoined in pairs. Man and woman, who represent the crown and glory of all created beings, in whom are embodied all the lower orders, were and are still created to associate in pairs—each created for the other, the one to help the other; the two to love and to belong to one another. This principle, fully carried out,

13

justifies and shows the necessity for the creation of man and woman precisely as they are, having bodies, parts and passions, will and understanding. It is my intention in the following pages to explain the relations existing between the sexes, for the purpose of showing that the greatest happiness to the human race will be found in living a life in full accord with these relations. In order that the subject may be fully understood, let us examine the physical development of man and woman in detail, particularizing the different organs of the body as they appear in their order of formation, from the very inmost or beginning, to the ultimate or end, in their respective natures.

Ever since the primal creation of man and woman, the human race has been perpetuated by a series of births. Children have been conceived in harmony with the natural order of events, in such matters, and have been born boys and girls. A boy is a boy to all intents and purposes from his very conception, from the very earliest moment of his being; begotten by his father he is a boy in embryo within the ovule of his mother. The converse is true of the opposite sex. At this very early age of reproduction the embryo has all the elements of the future man or woman, mentally and physically, even before any form becomes apparent; and so small is the human being at the earliest stage of its existence that no material change is observable between the ovule that contains the product of conception and a fully developed ovule unimpregnated.*

It is about twelve days after conception before the impregnated ovule, which undergoes many changes during this time, makes its escape from the ovary where it became impregnated and enters one of the Fallopian tubes, thence gradually descending into the cavity of the womb. Here it begins to mature and become fitted for its birth into the outer world. Soon now the embryo (for such it is called at this early stage) begins to assume form. The first indication of formation that it is possible to discover, even by the help of the microscope, consists of an oblong figure, obtuse at one extremity, swollen in the middle, blunt-pointed at the other extremity. The rudimentary embryo is slightly curved forward, is of a grayish white color, of a gelatinous consistence, from two to four lines long and weighs one or two grains. A slight depression representing the neck, enables us to distinguish

* For fuller particulars see Guernsey's Obstetrics, 3d edition, pages 79–89, inclusive.

the head; the body is marked by a swollen centre, but there are as yet no traces of the extremities. So much can be observed about the end of the third week after conception.

At about the *fifth week* the embryo presents more distinctions. The head is very large in proportion to the rest of the body, the eyes are represented by two black spots, and the upper extremities by small protuberances on the sides of the trunk. The embryo at this stage is nearly two-thirds of an inch in length and weighs about fifteen grains. The lower extremities now begin to appear in the shape of two minute rounded tubercles. Till about this time a straight artery has been observed to beat with the regularity of the pulse; but now it appears doubled somewhat into the shape of an adult heart, although as yet it has but one auricle and one ventricle. As time advances we find the perfect heart with its two ventricles and two auricles, all developed from the original straight artery. At this period the lungs appear to exist in five or six different lobes and we can barely distinguish the bronchial tubes; about the same time the ears and face are distinctly outlined, and after awhile the nose is also faintly and imperfectly perceived.

At about the *seventh week* a little bony deposit is found in the lower jaw. The kidneys now begin to be formed, and a little later the genital organs. The embryo averages one inch in length.

At *two months* the rudiments of the extremities become more prominent. The forearm and hand can be distinguished but not the arm above the elbow; the hand is larger than the forearm, but is not supplied with fingers. The sex cannot yet be determined. The length of the embryo is from one inch and a half to two inches, and it weighs from three to five drachms. The eyes are discernible, but still uncovered by the rudimentary lids. The nose forms an obtuse eminence, the nostrils are rounded and separated, the mouth is gaping and the epidermis can be distinguished from the true skin.

At *ten weeks* the embryo is from one and a half to two and a half inches long, and its weight is from one ounce to an ounce and a half, the eyelids are more developed and descend in front of the eyes; the mouth begins to be closed by the development of the lips. The walls of the chest are more completely formed, so that it is no longer possible to see the movements of the heart. The fingers become distinct and the toes appear as small projections webbed together like a frog's foot. At about this period the sexual organs show their development as follows: On each side of the urinary locality an oblong fold becomes distinguishable; in course of progress if these folds remain separate, a little tubercle forms in the anterior commissure which becomes the clitoris; the nymphæ develop, the urethra forms between them, and the female sex is determined. If, on the other hand, these folds unite into a rounded projection the scrotum is formed, the little tubercle above becomes the penis and hence the male sex. The testicles forming within the body, descend later into the scrotum, and organs similar to them, their counterparts, form in the female and are called ovaries. These ovaries are found attached to an organ called the womb, and this again is united with the vagina, which leads downwards and outwards between the labia majora.*

At the end of the *third month* the weight of the embryo is from three to four ounces and its length from four to five inches, the eyeballs are seen through the lids, the pupils of the eyes are discernible, the forehead, nose and lips can be clearly distinguished. The finger nails resemble thin membranous plates, the skin shows more firmness, but is still rosy-

---

* For fuller particulars see Guernsey's Obstetrics.

hued, thin and transparent. The sex can now be fully determined.

At the end of the *fourth month* the product of conception is no longer called an embryo, but a fœtus. The body is from six to eight inches in length and weighs six or seven ounces. A few little white hairs are seen scattered over the scalp. The development of the face is still imperfect. The eyes are now closed by their lids, the nostrils are well-formed, the mouth is shut in by the lips and the sex is still more sharply defined. The tongue may be observed far back in the mouth, and the lower part of the face is rounded off by what a little later will be a well-formed chin. The movements of the fœtus are by this time plainly felt by the mother, and if born at this time it may live several months.

At the end of the *fifth month* the body of the fœtus is from seven to nine inches long and weighs from eight to eleven ounces. The skin has a fairer appearance and more consistence; the eyes can no longer be distinguished through the lids, owing to the increased thickness of the latter. The head, heart and kidneys are large and well developed. At the end of the *sixth month* the fœtus is from eleven to twelve and a half inches in length, and weighs about sixteen ounces, more or less. The hair upon the scalp is thicker and longer, the eyes remain closed, and very delicate hairs may be seen upon the margins of the eye-lids and upon the eye-brows. The nails are solid, the scrotum small and empty, the surface of the skin appears wrinkled but the dermis may be distinguished from the epidermis. The liver is large and red, and the gall-bladder contains fluid.

At the end of the *seventh month* the length of the fœtus is from twelve and a half to fourteen inches, its weight is about fifty-five ounces, and it is both well defined and well proportioned in all its parts. The bones of the cranium, hitherto quite flat, now appear a little arched, and as the process of ossification goes on, the arching increases till the vault is quite complete. The brain presents greater firmness, and the eye-lids are opened. The skin is much firmer and red. The gall-bladder contains bile.

At the end of the *eighth month* the fœtus seems to thicken up rather than to increase in length, since it is only from sixteen to eighteen inches long while its weight increases from four to five pounds. The skin is red, and characterized at this period by a fine downy covering, over which is spread a quantity of thick viscous matter, called the sebaceous coat, which has been forming since the latter part of the fifth month. The lower jaw has now become as long as the upper one, and in the male the left testicle may be found in the scrotum. Convolutions appear in the brain structure.

At *nine months* the anxious time of parturition has arrived. The fœtus is from nineteen to twenty-three inches in length and weighs on an average from six to eight pounds. Children at birth sometimes weigh as much as fourteen pounds; but such extremes are very rare. At this period the white and grey matter of the brain are distinct, and the convolutions are well marked; the nails assume a horny consistence, hair upon the head is more or less abundant, the testes are in the scrotum, and the entire external genital organs of both male and female are well formed.

The above particulars respecting the development of the human being have been narrated to show that one organ is just as important as another, and that each is really dependent upon the other; no one could exist without the other and all are to subserve a use. First must be the *esse* (the inmost) the vital force imparted to the ovule. A little

later certain changes take place in the ovule,
later still other changes, and finally about the
fifteenth day a slight development of the new
human being can just be outlined by the help
of the microscope, which, as before stated, has
form at about the third week after conception.
First the vestige of a head and body, a little
later the heart and lungs appear lying in the
open chest; then the hands are protruded from
the sides of the trunk, afterwards the fore-
arms, then the arms, all pushed out from the
body; the feet and legs gradually protrude
from the lower end of the trunk, and the chest
closes. up so that the heart and lungs can no
longer be seen; the face, mouth and eyes take
form, the external genital organs make their
appearance in conjunction with other developments, and in due course of time the boy or
girl is born ready for further developments in childhood, and adolescence. When
the latter development has been attained, if
due care has been taken by all interested
parties, we have pure men and pure women
fitted to enter upon the privileges and the
uses of a wedded life according to the design
of our Creator.

How wonderfully and how instructively are
all organs in the animal body disposed and
arranged! In the highest place we find the

brain to govern and rule over all below. It is the first organ formed and in an orderly life should control all the others. Next in order and importance are the heart and lungs, which put into motion all other parts and enable the animal frame to continue in motion. So each and every organ is developed in its proper order, all to obey the commands of the first and most important—the brain, the seat of the reason and the will. Happy are they of either sex who will govern themselves by a pure enlightened reason and a pure affectionate will.

CHAPTER II.

The Infant.

Embracing the First Year of the Child's Life.

THE battle of life really begins as soon as the child is born. Its cleanliness, its clothing, its temperature and its food are matters for daily observance and care, as also are the light, sunshine and air which it is to breathe. Opiates, soothing syrups and cordials, are to be strictly avoided as being deleterious to health; proper sanitary measures usually suffice to render all *dosing* unnecessary. Spirituous potions and lotions should be avoided as being contrary to the laws of hygiene as well as for fear the child may learn to love and to become addicted to their use later in life. Every organ of the body should be carefully protected even at this early age, so that health may reign supreme. Particular care and the utmost solicitude should be bestowed upon the genital organs. No rubbing or handling of these parts should be permitted under any pretense whatever— beyond what may be absolutely necessary for cleanliness. The genital organs require just

24

as much watchful care, if not more, as the
stomach, the eye, the ear, &c. I regret to
say that I have known some fathers to tickle
the genital organs of their infant boys until a
complete erection of the little penis ensued,
which effect pleases the father as an evidence
of a robust boy. The evil effects of such a
procedure are too manifest to require dilating
upon. Fathers take warning !

Nurses are known to quiet young children
by gently exciting pleasurable sensations
about the genital organs both of males and
females—practices which are the most vicious
and vice-begetting that can possibly be in-
vented. Many a young man and young
woman has fallen to very low depths from
influences developed by these and similar
means. Nurses should be cautioned in this
matter *and carefully watched too*, as even the
least suspected may (innocently perhaps) be
guilty of this fault to save themselves the
trouble of quieting their charges in a proper
way. Early impressions upon these animal
passions, as well as those made upon other
senses of the young, are very abiding. Mothers be watchful !

Great care should be exercised in the
choice of a diaper for infants and the material
of which it is made. The diaper should fit

easily about the organs which it covers and
protects, so as not to cause undue heating or
friction of the parts; and immediately after a
babe has soiled itself either with urine or
from a motion of the bowels, it should be
made clean and dry at once to avoid any irritation that would otherwise ensue upon these
delicate parts. The material of which the
diaper is made should not be stiff or harsh,
but very limp, soft and pliable; nor should it
be thick and bungling. There are great objections to the use of oil-cloth, rubber or other
impervious materials as they prevent the escape of perspiration, urine, fecal matter, etc.
As soon as possible, say near the end of the
first year, the child should be taught to use
its little chair-commode, thus dispensing with
the diaper at an early age. This is much
better for the sexual organs, is more comfortable for the child and is more healthy; it also
favors a more perfect development of the
limbs and joints, the hip joints particularly.

CHAPTER III.

CHILDHOOD.

CHILDHOOD is that portion of life ex-
tending from infancy to adolescence,
which in boys occurs at the age of fourteen to sixteen years; and in girls at the age
of twelve to fourteen years. In very warm
climates adolescence is reached some two
or three years earlier.

Most fortunate the infant who has completed
its term of life, thus far, in accordance with the
strictest rules of Hygiene, or the laws of health.

"In a state of health sexual impressions
should never affect a child's mind or body.
All its vital energy should be employed in
constructing the growing frame, in storing up
proper external impressions and in educating
the brain to receive them." Unfortunately
this state of health is not always attained.
Impressions may be exhibited in these organs
at a very early age either from inheritance,
from improper handling or from some morbid condition of the child that could show
itself in no other organ of the body and
which, like morbid conditions in general,

27

make their appearance somewhere in the mind or body.

SEXUAL PRECOCITY.—Many parents who are most particular in all other respects, as to the moral and physical training of their children, imagine there is no need to pay any special attention to the genital organs. This, however, is a grave mistake and needs our careful consideration. As is well known, some children evince a sexual precocity which may lead to very serious results. In these it often happens that the sexual instinct arises long before puberty; such children, if males, manifest an instinctive attraction towards the female sex which they show by constantly spying after their nurses, chambermaids, etc.; by seeking as much as possible to play with children of the opposite sex and improperly toying with them. *"One case is so remarkable that an abstract of it may be instructive: M. D——, between five and six years of age, was one day in summer in the room of a dressmaker who lived in the family; this girl thinking that she might put herself at ease before such a child, threw herself on her bed, almost without clothing. The little D—— had followed all her motions and regarded her figure with a greedy eye. He

* Lallemand and Wilson, page 140.

approached her on the bed, as if to sleep, but soon became so bold in his behavior that the girl, after having laughed at him for some time was obliged to put him out of the room. This girl's simple imprudence produced such an impression on the child that forty years afterwards he had not forgotten a single circumstance connected with it."

Parents are remarkably careless on this point. They allow children to play together for hours at a time without the surveillance of an older person, provided only they are removed from any danger. It is sufficient to merely draw attention to such a custom as every reflective mind can easily draw the inevitable consequences. Habits are indulged in and marks of familiarity shown which should not for an instant be tolerated.

CAUSES which commonly produce sexual impressions on young children are, allowing them to repose playfully on their belly, to slide down bannisters, to go too long without urinating, constipation or straining at stool, cutaneous affections and worms. Also, thoughtless acts of elder people which are very frequently more closely observed than is commonly supposed. The sliding down bannisters produces a titillation which is agreeable to the sexual organs. Children of both sexes will constantly repeat this act until they learn to become inveterate masturbators, even at a very early age.

Among boys a disease called *priapism* is often developed; this arises from undue handling of the parts, or from some morbid state of the child's health. The disorder consists of paroxysms, occurring more or less frequently, of violent erections of the penis; these sometimes become very painful and require the attention of a physician. At all events medical aid should be sought at once, because some functional derangement is at work which might, if not arrested and cured, give rise to masturbation. Owing to unknown causes such morbid conditions induce some little boys to pull frequently at the foreskin of the penis until their health is seriously impaired; they pine away, lose flesh, and still continue to worry at the foreskin, till death has been known to result. These cases require the most careful and skillful constitutional treatment, until they are cured.

Sometimes, in other cases, the foreskin becomes inflamed, offensive secretions may form about the end of the penis, etc. . All such disorders should be submitted to a judicious physician at once, to avoid irritations which might result in a tendency to sexual excitement—a calamity truly deplorable to the young. The idea which some writers advance—that a long prepuce (or foreskin) often proves an exciting cause of troublesome sensations to the boy, is certainly erroneous. So, too, it is all wrong to state that particular care should be taken to wash under the prepuce. That this objection in regard to washing is true, is proved from the physical fact that in a large majority of boys the orifice of the foreskin is not sufficiently opened to permit of these washings. And the objection is still further proved by the fact that all these unnatural secretions, offensive odors, sensations, etc., which irritate and worry a boy, together with all inflamations of these parts are soon relieved and permanently cured by the proper medicament. Needless laving, handling or rubbing the sexual parts should be avoided as strictly as possible. To show how little good such washings really do, even though persisted in, I will mention one out of many similar cases: "In spite of repeated washings every day, a fetid smegma was deposited in considerable quantity on the glans, causing a tiresome burning and itching." All such cases are utterly intractable by any amount of bathing. But the suitable remedy administered internally cures the trouble per-

manently in a few weeks and at the same
time improves the general tone and health of
the individual. This is so because the proper
remedy removes the morbific cause which
produced that condition of the penis and all
concomitant symptoms, at the same time. It
must be remembered that the troubles referred
to above come from within, and that they are
but developments of internal morbific causes.
In a similar manner, small pox, measles,
chicken pox and all eruptive diseases come
out as products from morbific causes *within.*
No sane person ever thinks of washing off
these appearances with the hope of curing
the case!

All our external parts were made just as
they should be and they work in harmony so
long as we are perfectly healthy inwardly.
Every blemish upon the skin, even to a wart,
has a corresponding morbid influence within,
which can be removed by proper treatment.
Let it be remembered then for all coming
time that a little boy's penis is never to be
meddled or trifled with, nor his foreskin, nor
the parts about the generative organs. All unnatural conditions, appearances or sensations
require prompt and proper medical aid. If
erections of his little penis occur during sleep,
or if he cannot urinate promptly on rising in

the morning, because of an erection, let these conditions beget an anxiety for his welfare and at once seek a judicious physician, who will be able to prescribe a medicament to arrest all further development of sexual precocity—an affliction so baneful to the young.

A little later in life children are liable to ascarides or seat worms, called by some "pin worms." No applications, purgatives, "vermifuges," injections or other mechanical means should ever be employed to remove these, as they are of constitutional origin and should be so treated, until perfectly cured. Removing the worms by irritants or by mechanical means does not remove the *cause* of their existence or reproduction in the body. The dyscrasia that gives rise to these worms, with the accompanying itching and tickling, is apt to cause a sexual excitement which may prove more disastrous than the original trouble itself. Therefore be sure that this affection is treated constitutionally; so long as the vital forces work in harmonious order, no abnormal appearances of any kind can come to light, because they do not exist.

From the age of nine to fourteen, boys generally acquire very curious notions about sexual affairs and are naturally, from what they hear, desirous of obtaining some idea

2*

of sexual congress, a knowledge of where
babies come from, etc. This curiosity, of
course, causes the mind to dwell much upon
sexual subjects. I fully believe that good
information will, by satisfying this curiosity,
free the mind to a great extent from sexual
thoughts. It is from such very thoughts that
boys are led to play with their sexual organs
in secret, and to handle them so as to excite
pleasurable sensations; erections of the penis
are thus produced and finally, by this contin-
ual excitation with the hand, the heighth of
sexual orgasm is reached, ejaculation of
semen occurs and *self-pollution* is the consequence. This act is called "masturbation"
and becomes a *secret vice of the worst kind!*

Very frequently and to an alarming extent
"masturbation" is taught by older boys, and
by young men even, in nearly all our colleges,
boarding, public and private schools, and by
companions under the paternal roof. This
act is repeated time after time until the de-
grading and destructive (morally and physically so) habit is confirmed. As a result, the
boy grows thin, pale, morose and passionate;
then weak, indolent and indifferent; his digestion becomes impaired, his sleep short, dis-
turbed and broken; he sometimes becomes
epileptic or falls into a state of marasmus; in

any case he is in great danger of being totally ruined forever.

There is a great difference in boys regarding the formation of these habits. While some may almost insensibly glide into them, others, intuitively as it were, turn away from all such temptations and banish all thoughts of a sexual nature from their minds at once. This is right. So long as a boy's mind refuses to harbor such baleful approaches, so long he is safe; but the moment he heeds them and allows them to enter his mind, that moment he is in danger and will most likely fall into bad habits. He must strenuously resist all such thoughts and going to his father or mother tell them about his trials and temptations and strive to forget them until success crowns his efforts. By persistent efforts, by repeated prayers to the Lord for help, by reading his Bible and good, pure stories, by running into the open air and indulging in some useful occupation or joyous, healthful play, he will eventually conquer them and thus rise to the dignity of a true man. Sometimes, too, it may be necessary to consult the physician for help. In addition to the instinctive shrinking which every right minded person generally feels from putting ideas of impurity into a child's innocent mind, a parent's pride leads him to hope that *his* boy would not indulge in any such mean and disgusting practices. But, bearing in mind the advice of Herbert Spencer—"that the aim of discipline should be to produce a *self-governing* being," the best advice a parent or guardian can, and ought, to give, is: do not harbor bad thoughts or feelings about anything; at once turn them away and think of something else, of something good, true and pure. Indulge in no hatred or revengeful feelings towards others; plot no evil things; always be true to your word, faithful to your duties and charitable to all. Treat everybody kindly and politely. And further, a child should be *taught* what "chastity" really is, instead of leaving him to find it out as best he may.

It should be clearly explained to him that true chastity requires the shunning of all indecency and foul language; that he should refrain from touching his secret parts except when the necessities of nature require it; that all sexual emotions should be subjugated. When he grows older every boy should be taught that chastity means continence; and it should be firmly impressed upon his mind that all lascivious actions are a drain upon his whole system and weaken the powers which the Lord has given him to be employed *only* in the married state. These are characteristics of a true man and will help him very much to keep out of sexual difficulties which, as we shall see further on, are among the greatest curses of life.

The use of tobacco, wine, coffee or tea by children is well known to be highly injurious. Never allow a child to use either of these—not even in small quantities. A too common practice in many families is to allow a little wine at dinner "to assist digestion!" Others allow coffee or tea, "because my child is so fond of it." "The after-effects of all these is to disturb the heart, to cause nervousness and irritability, and *to weaken the sexual organs in a marked degree.* Tobacco particularly has this last effect in old and young, besides producing convulsions, a dulled intellect, etc."*

Remember where the brain is and the purposes for which it has been given! Here reside the knowledge and the power to govern all below it. No matter what the stomach craves or how strongly the appetite begs for this or that; no matter how much one may be tempted to steal, to lie or to swear; no matter how much the sexual organs may lead one to think about or handle them—here is

* Lallemand and Wilson.

the great and good brain, the home of the
will-power, which says: "Touch not, taste
not, handle not." So long as these commands
are listened to and obeyed, one is safe. The
desire need not and should not control the
act—but the rational faculty can and will control, when early taught to do so. The more
one is led by this rational faculty the easier
it becomes to follow it, and *vice versa.*

What has been said above regarding the
danger of little boys falling into bad habits
applies with equal force to little girls. Do
not forget this. They too may have sexual
thoughts, feelings and curiosity, and care
must be taken to keep their minds pure and
bodies healthy. They are also liable to disorders that require prompt and careful attention, such as inflamations, excoriations, itch-
ings and swellings of the genital organs with
discharges from these parts resembling leucorrhœa. All such conditions lead them to
more or less rub and scratch these parts—
which should never be touched—for relief.
Pleasurable sensations are experienced and
then comes masturbation—*a sin chargeable to
the parent* for not having given the matter
proper medical attention. "Repeated washings" will no more cure these cases in little
girls than, as shown above, will they cure in

little boys. All these are but the outcropping of some constitutional affection and should be treated accordingly. No applications or medicated washings of any kind should be allowed. Such external treatment only palliates the suffering for a little while without removing the disorded vital force that gave origin to its appearance. This is simply repressed and may react upon the child and appear in another form tenfold worse than the first. The passing of urine or fecal matter may (in either sex) cause irritation and excoriation; this is another sign that all is not right in the vital forces and should be mentioned to the physician as a sure index that medical treatment. but not topical applications, is absolutely necessary. All abnormal appearances, actions and discomforts of the child, whether mental or physical, should be submitted to an experienced and judicious physician. A healthy child should be **happy** and comfortable in all respects.

A very successful plan for keeping children from vice or vicious habits is to see that their time is fully occupied with amusements and duties which interest them. They need a great deal of harmlessly conducted amusement and—do *not* strive to "keep them quiet." Allow little boys and girls to play together, under proper surveillance, and let them be boisterous if they will; let them romp and run, climb fences, trundle hoops, jump rope, go to dancing school, participate in military drills, go coasting and skating, take swimming lessons, etc.

No judicious parents will allow a son or daughter to be alone much; to seek to be alone is always a bad sign and should be carefully guarded against without its being known that such precaution is observed. Furnish them liberally with instructive and innocent story books and let them read aloud to you or to each other. Take them to walk or ride when you go, and strive to make companions of them as much as possible, making whatever sacrifices are necessary to attain this end. Above all, *encourage their making confidants of you.* Let them feel that they can come and talk freely on any subject, no matter what its nature may be. Do this, and you have thrown around them a bulwark of defence that will withstand the repeated attacks of hosts of evil spirits. When night comes and they go to bed, let them learn to go to sleep at once; no play then—they may be read to sleep, but no romping or playing. No strange children should be allowed to sleep with yours; make them occupy separate rooms or at least separate beds; be sure that the sleeping places of your children are sacred to them alone. Nor is it advisable for children to sleep with a grown person of either sex and particularly not with servants—all for obvious reasons.

The observance of all these precautions against influences that might excite sexual disturbance is most sacred in its character and most needful even in a religious point of view; for there should be *chastity* above all things.

CHAPTER IV.

ADOLESCENCE OF THE MALE.

ADOLESCENCE of the male embraces the period of life from the age of fourteen or sixteen years to the age of twenty-five.

At about the age of fourteen years " the period of youth is distinguished by that advance in the evolution of the generative apparatus in both sexes, and by that acquirement of its power of functional activity, which constitutes the state of *Puberty.*" At this age the following great changes take place in the general appearance and deportment of the male : His frame becomes more angular and the masculine proportions more pronounced ; increased strength and greater powers of endurance are manifested ; the larynx enlarges and the voice becomes lower in pitch as well as rougher and more powerful ; new feelings and desires awaken in the mind. His deportment becomes more commanding, his frivolity is less and less apparent, and the boy is lost in the man. If he has been so fortunate as to escape all the dangers

42

and baneful influences of childhood, he is manly indeed, and we behold him with an unburdened conscience, bright intellect, frank address and good memory. His spirits are buoyant and his complexion clear; every function of his body is well performed, and no fatigue is felt after moderate exertion. He evinces that elasticity of body, and that happy control of himself and his feelings, which are indicative of the robust health and absence of care which should accompany youth. His time is devoted to his studies, duties and amusements; as he feels his stature increase, and his intellect enlarge, he gladly prepares for his coming struggle with the world.

All boys may come to this condition with proper training through the period of infancy and childhood; and after arriving at the adolescent age of their existence as they have the power of mind to *choose*, so also have they the power to *refuse*. The human race is created above the animal so that we are something more than mere animals; we are human beings with human propensities, human passions, human desires and human tastes, which are subject to the human brain, to the human reason and to the human will—all elevated and ennobled by the Divine Will. Man must not let himself down to be governed by animal passions; the moment he does that, his higher powers suffer and become weakened, and he becomes more like an inferior animal; if he persists in this downward course, his lower powers become strengthened until finally they transcend and rule the higher. Then, to all intents and purposes, such a man's head is downwards and the lower part of his body is upwards just where his head ought to be.

Man is a human being, yet, like the whole animal kingdom, he has appetites, desires and passions, as it is absolutely necessary that he should have. He has organs corresponding to these appetites, desires and passions, and it is necessary that he should have them. A proper understanding in regard to this matter will convince anyone of the truth of this assertion. Our Creator doeth all things wisely and well, in the most perfect manner possible. Consequently, man with all his organs, parts and passions is just what he should be when he blossoms into youth, in the perfection of his adolescence as described above. In fact there could be no other form of creating man, for the Lord always creates in the most perfect way possible, according to one harmonious law which He has ordained to govern the creation of all beings.

Such a man is fully prepared to struggle
with himself and the world at large. In his
desires, appetites or passions of any kind, he,
in his humanity, protected by his rational
faculties and enlightened by the Divine
Oracle of God, unquestionably has the power
to choose between propriety and impropriety,
between the right and the wrong, between the
good and the bad. Take any evil into which
a member of the human family may fall—the
love of ardent spirit for instance; he first
thinks of it and desires to partake of some.
Finally he takes an opportunity to gratify his
desire, does satisfy it for the time and thinks
it very nice. The next craving is a little
more intense, and he cannot overcome the
temptation quite so easily as he could have
done before, and at last he indulges again.
So he goes on, step by step, until he may fall
very low. *The same thinking, feeling and
desiring preceeds the adoption of every vicious
habit that was ever formed.* Nor will anyone
pretend to say that a persistent effort of the
will power, at the very outset, when he first
perceived the tendencies of his desires to do
what he need not do, would not have prevented
the evil; no argumentation will prevail in the
face of stubborn facts, and the real facts are
all on the side of purity and order.

These very young men or youths, as they
progress through adolescence, may become
tempted in a variety of ways, some to the use of
ardent spirits or tobacco, others to lie, to steal,
to forge, &c.; but the approach to all these
evils is gradual and first comes through the
mind. They first think about the action, turn
it over and over in their minds until .they
come to greatly desire and then, later, to
commit the evil which would not have been
ultimated if the mind had been persistently
set against it in the beginning. This is an
indisputable fact.

In this manner many promising youths,
just as they are blossoming into the pride of
early manhood, begin to indulge in sexual
thoughts and to allow these thoughts to
influence their minds until they commit some
of the evils to which perverted and unchaste
passions lead them. If this evil be masturbation,
then they are on the direct road to ruin, as
will be seen described further on. If it be
the commission of sexual intercourse with
women, their ruin is still more certain, and in
the latter case they are exposed to one of the
worst poisons that can possibly infect the
human race. I do not overdraw the picture
when I declare that *millions of human beings
die annually from the effects of poison*

contracted in this way, in some form of suffering or another; for, by insinuating its effects
into and poisoning the whole man, it compli-
cates various disorders and renders them
incurable. When gonorrhœa is contracted,
although frequently suppressed by local treatment in the form of injections, it is never perfectly cured thereby. No; the hidden poison
runs on for a life time producing strictures,
dysuria, gleet and kindred diseases; finally, in
old men, a horrible prostatitis results from
which the balance of one's life is rendered
miserable indeed. If inflammation of the lungs
supervenes, there is often a translation of the
virus to these al organs, causing what is
termed "plastic pneumonia," where one
lobule after another becomes gradually sealed
up, till nearly the whole of both lungs
becomes impervious to air, and death results
from asphyxia.

This horrible infection sometimes becomes
engrafted upon other acute diseases when
lingering disorders follow, causing years of
misery, and only terminating in death.

If real syphilis, in the form of chancre,
should be contracted, and in that form suppressed, we have buboes often of a malignant
type, ulceration of the penis and a loss of
some portion of this member. Sometimes

the poison attacks the throat, causing most
destructive ulcerations therein ; sometimes it
seizes upon the nasal bones, resulting in their
entire destruction and an awful disfiguration
of the face; sometimes it ultimates itself in
the ulceration and destruction of other
osseous tissues in different portions of the
body. Living examples of these facts are too
frequently witnessed in the streets of any
large city. Young men marrying with the
slightest taint of this poison in the blood will
surely transmit the disease to their children.
Thousands of abortions transpire every year
from this cause alone, the poison being so
destructive as to kill the child *in utero*, before
it is matured for birth; and even if the child
be born alive, it is liable to break down with
the most loathsome disorders of some kind
and to die during dentition; the few that
survive this period are short lived and are
unhealthy so long as they do live. The very
first unchaste connection of a man with a
woman may be attended with a contamination
entailing upon him a life of suffering and
even death itself. There is no safety among
impure or loose women whether in private
homes or in the very best regulated houses of
ill-fame; even in Paris, where, after women have
been carefully examined and pronounced

free from any infecting condition, the first
man who visits one of them, often carries
away a deadly enemy in his blood, which had
lurked in concealment beyond the keen eye
of the inspector. A young man, or a man at
any age, is in far greater danger amidst
company of this stamp, than he would
be with a clear conscience and pure character in the midst of the wildest forest,
full of all manner of poisonous serpents and
wild beasts of every description. A knowledge
of the above facts should be enough to chill the
first impulse and to make any man who
respects his own well-being, turn away and
flee from the destruction that awaits him.

As if the above sufferings were not a
sufficient penalty for the transgression
against the law—" Be ye pure," we find yet
another. Coincident with the physical wreck,
which syphilis makes of the man who
becomes thoroughly tainted with its poison,
comes his moral wreck. He loses all respect
for the truth and all regard for his word; no
dependence of any kind can be placed upon
him, and he will not pay his debts or fulfil
any moral obligation; all because he began
by prostituting his mind more and more until,
with deadened conscience, almost literally,
his head is dependent and his feet uppermost,

ruling all the better part of his nature. And next come the mental sufferings—and most agonizing they are. Unhappy to the last degree, he no longer takes pleasure in life, but, wishing to die, finally commits suicide. A search in any insane asylum will show that a very large proportion of patients are made up from those who masturbate or have syphilis. Stamp out these two evils, or rather *curses* of the human race, and the supply that feeds our insane asylums, aye and our penitentiaries, too, will become vastly lessened. Think of it! So many of the inhabitants of our prisons, asylums, and our poor-houses, are composed of men and women who have offended against nature's laws by violating their own sexual nature. Add to this summary the list of broken hearted, deflowered virgins and unwedded mothers, and you have the picture complete.

What a contrast with that manliness of character from which he has fallen! Now he is in an insane condition, blaming everyone for having contributed to his many misfortunes and his fallen condition, whereas he alone is the culprit. No one made him commit the first or any subsequent evil. He allowed his own mind to yield to the first temptation, and then went on from step to step, he alone being responsible for the result. Yield not the first point, and all is safe.

The pride of perfect adolescence, as described a few pages back, is due to purity of thought, to chastity and continence. This purity shines through every tissue, enkindles the eye with a true expression, makes bright the countenance and erects the form. It gives elasticity to the step, causes harmony in the tones of the voice, and adds dignity to the carriage and deportment. The first step in the paths of vice in any form, whether in sexual errors or any other, detracts in the exact degree of the digression from all of the above beautiful and ennobling characteristics.

We have spoken in the preceding pages of new feelings and desires being awakened in the youth after his fourteenth year. This change is wholly due to his approaching manhood, to the time when he will be fully prepared to appreciate, to love and protect, guide and support her whom he makes his wife, and to become the father of happy and healthy children. But this approach to manhood is not due to the development of the genital organs, as some writers affirm, for this would be a reversion of orderly development. The approaching manhood develops in full accordance to their uses and importance *all* the organs belonging to man. As the well-developed infant has all its organs developed in a condition suitable for its state, and the child has all its organs in all parts of the body, developed in full accord with its state, so adolescence follows, and every organ must develop accordingly; and in this develop-ment a new impetus is given to every organ in the body. The whole man awakens to a newness of life as is seen in the change of his voice, the spreading out of his frame, the independence and command of his bearing, the activity of his brain, the soundness of his judgment, until he becomes in the fullest sense a rational being. Of course the devel-opment of his genital organs keeps pace with that of his brain; but the brain should lead the way throughout the entire development of the human race.

At the time of puberty, then, a new and a different sensation springs up in the generative organs, which is in perfect harmony with the uses for which they are intended. We recog-nize the use of the hands, the fingers, the feet, the eyes, the ears, the sense of taste, &c., and we use them accordingly. We should think of the generative organs only in the same light. They are intended for use, for the highest and holiest use of procreating human beings to the end that they may become angels in heaven. These organs were not made to be abused; but they are abused every time the mind is allowed to dwell upon them improperly. Every excitation we allow from lewd thoughts or fancies, has a debasing and deteriorating effect upon that well-developed form, upon that conscience so free, and upon that countenance so open and bright, which has been described in the preceding pages.

If the mere thought and excitation arising therefrom are injurious to the perfection of the youth, how much more injurious must be the ultimation of that thought in masturbation, in unlawful sexual intercourse, or in the loss of seminal fluid by other unnatural means.

Right here I feel impelled to say something of the

DIFFICULTY OF MAINTAINING CHASTITY.

I, in connection with many of our best and wisest men who have given the subject a lifetime's most earnest consideration, hold that for a young man whose early education has been carefully looked to, and consequently, whose mind has not been debased by vile practices, it is no more impossible mentally, or injurious physically, to preserve his chastity than to refrain from yielding to any other of the innumerable temptations with which his life is beset. And every year of voluntary chastity renders the task easier by mere force of habit. I wish to be clearly understood in this matter.

So long as a young man remains chaste in thought and deed, he will not suffer any bad effects from his continence. It is the *semi-continent*, the man who knows the right but pursues the wrong, who suffers! Patients frequently complain that enforced continence makes them restless, irritable, unfit for mental application of any sort, &c. Sexual intercourse is then indulged in, and presto: for the time being, what a welcome change. The now unclogged mind grasps with vigor any subject presented to it, the spirits are exuberant and the physical frame buoyant. But, is the trouble cured, is it permanently eradicated from the system? No! In a short time the symptoms reappear and the same remedy is again sought. The more the sexual feelings are indulged the more frequent will be their recurrence, and the result need not be written; every candid mind can easily see it. To their shame and confusion be it said, there are many physicians who, when consulted by their patients for medical assistance in such trials, "deliberately encourage the early indulgence of the passions, on the false and wicked ground that self-restraint is incompatible with health. What abhorrence can be too deep for a doctrine so destructive, or for the teachers who thus, before the eyes of those whose youthful ignorance, whose sore natural temptation, rather call for the wisest and tenderest guidance and encouragement, put darkness for light, evil for good, and bitter for sweet." *

I declare emphatically that no symptoms of sexual suffering, no matter how feelingly described or cunningly insinuated, should ever lead a physician to prescribe for a young man that fatal remedy, illicit intercourse. Medically as a physician, morally as a Christian, and sympathizingly as a fellow being, I record a solemn protest against such false treatment. It is better for a youth to live a continent life. The strictly chaste suffer comparatively little sexual irritability; but the incontinent, at recurring periods are sure to be troubled in one or other of the ways spoken of; and the remedy of indulgence, if effective, requires repetition as often as the inconvenience returns. No! When thus consulted, let the physician prescribe the

* Wm. Acton, M. R. C. S.

proper medicament, if one be necessary;
and let him direct a plain, nourishing, non-
stimulating diet, physical exertion of any
kind carried to exhaustion, and SELF CON-
TROL.

Would any young man in his senses listen
to a physician, who, for lowness of spirits,
mental despondency, &c., should tell him to
drink plentifully of brandy or eat hasheesh?
On the same principle then let a youth shun
the physician, who, for sexual excitement,
prescribes sexual indulgence.

Again, such complaints coming from young
men are very often specious, and are mere
subterfuges—overdrawn pictures of their sufferings—which are presented as an excuse for
indulging the sensual emotions, instead of
manfully and righteously struggling to overcome them. And further, "if anyone wishes
to really experience the acutest sexual suffering, he can adopt no more certain method
than to be incontinent with the intention
of becoming continent again, when he has
'sown his wild oats.' The agony of breaking
off a habit which so rapidly entwines itself
with every fibre of the human frame (as
sexual indulgence) is such that it would not
be too much to say in the Wise Man's
words, '*None* that go to her return again,

neither take they hold on the paths of life.'"
> "The sin, of all, most sure to blight—
> The sin, of all, that the soul's light
> Is soonest lost, extinguished in."

Remember then that sexual suffering comes to the *incontinent* man, and that it is far easier, even for the fully developed vigorous adult, to continue in control of these feelings, than when they have been once excited and indulged.

One single impure connection may entail a whole life of syphilitic suffering on the unhappy transgressor. Would this "pay?"

No inducement could persuade me to assume the awful responsibilities of advising illicit intercourse. Apart from Christian principle, I know that there is no necessity, physiological, pathological or any other, that can excuse any physician for saying that the Seventh Commandment may ever be broken. My sentiments on the physiological side of the question are so admirably expressed by Acton,* that I will here quote from him.

"One argument in favor of incontinence deserves special notice, as it purports to be founded on physiology. I have been consulted by persons who feared, or professed to fear, that if the organs were not exercised regu-

---

* Fourth American Edition, P. 97.

larly, they would become atrophied, or that in some way impotence might be the result of chastity. This is the assigned reason for committing fornication. There exists *no greater* error than this, or one more opposed to physiological truth. In the first place, I may state that I have, after many years' experience, never seen a single instance of atrophy of the generative organs from this cause. I have, it is true, met with the complaint—but in what class of cases does it occur? It arises in all instances from the exactly opposite cause — abuse: the organs become worn out, and hence arises atrophy. Physiologically considered, it is not a fact that the power of secreting semen is annihilated in well-formed adults leading a healthy life and yet remaining continent. The function goes on in the organ always, from puberty to old age. Semen is secreted sometimes slowly, sometimes quickly, and very frequently under the influence of the will. No continent man need be deterred by this apocryphal fear of atrophy of the testes from living a chaste life. It is a device of the unchaste—a lame excuse for their own incontinence, unfounded on any physiological law. The testes will take care that their action is not interfered with."

Many and many a time have I heard it

regretted and bemoaned, on account of the many troubles they had seemed to cause, that the sexual organs exist. It is the lewd thoughts and uses to which they are put that causes all this misery, and there is always that "first thought" which should not be harbored. Cast away the impure thoughts, rise above them, and one is safe! Pure thoughts can *never* lead to harm.

The generative organs, with their functions and uses, are most closely interwoven with the highest destiny and well being of the race physically, mentally and spiritually; they are a part of us, without which there would be no men and women, lovers and loved ones, fathers and mothers, brothers and sisters. We must then happily accept the situation as it is, and our bodies, parts and passions as they are; for they are all indispensable, high and holy, when kept in an orderly and chaste condition. We only need the above knowledge and its application to make ourselves as happy in the enjoyment of these organs as it was designed by our Creator that we should be.

To rise above the sexual temptations that may be more or less experienced by many and perhaps by all, requires an effort of course, and frequently a very great effort;

but let it be borne in mind that all temptations
to do wrong, require effort to overcome them;
and as a rule, the greater the evil we are
tempted to commit the greater is the effort
needed to overcome it.   Now, as shown above,
since sexual matters are so thoroughly interwoven with the highest destinies of the human
race, physically, mentally and spiritually, there
is scarcely any function of higher import, allot-
ted to any individual, than that assigned to
the genital organs.   No function more deeply
concerns the healthfulness of the body, the
clearness and brilliancy of the intellect, or the
purity and sincerity of the soul itself.

Several times in the course of this book I
have referred to the term "abuse."   By "abuse,"
I mean precisely what *Lallemand* so forcibly
expresses as follows: "*I understand by the
term abuse, when applied to the organs of
generation, any irregular or premature exercise of their functions; any application of them
which cannot have, as its result, the propaga-
tion of the species.*"

Look at the habitual masturbator! See how
thin, pale and haggard he appears; how his
eyes are sunken; how long and cadaverous is his
cast of countenance; how irritable he is and how
sluggish, mentally and physically; how afraid
he is to meet the eye of his fellows; feel his

damp and chilling hand, so characteristic of great vital exhaustion. Taken as a class, how terrible are their lost virility, their miserable night's sleep, their convulsions and their shrunken limbs. They keep by themselves, seeking charm in solitude and are fit companions for no one; they dare not read their Bible, they cannot commune with good angels nor with the Lord, our Saviour. Is not this picture deplorable? It is at the last end of the chain I admit, but it is reached link after link, one at a time; and the first link was forged when the first temptation in the mind was first favored and finally yielded to. The above picture is a true one and shows how intimately connected are the soul, the mind and the body with this whole subject. Man in a healthy state need not and should not lose one drop of seminal fluid by his own hand, by nightly emissions or pollutions, or in any way, until he becomes conjoined to a wife of his choice in the holy bonds of matrimony. Every time the seed of his body is lost in a disorderly or unnatural way, he injures the finest textures of his brain correspondingly, as well as the finest and most exalted condition of his mind and soul, because the act proceeds in its incipiency from a willful prostitution of these higher powers.

When sexual thoughts and temptations arise in one's mind, even very young men are capable of putting them away, urged by the thought that tampering with one's generative organs is wrong. He should intuitively feel that it is something akin to theft, or a crime of some worse sort, for him to indulge in solitary vice and he should intuitively feel an inward reproach for all such meditations. When one is sorely tempted in these matters, as is often the case, let him reflect that he was not created to indulge in such pleasures by himself, and that to do so is a crime, a sin against the God of Heaven; that it is his destiny, his privilege and one of the uses of his life to share such enjoyments with the wife of his bosom; and that all excitement or dallying with this part of his nature before marriage only serves to weaken his sexual powers, as well as his mind and body; also, that it mars his sexual uses and will detract from his sexual pleasures in the married life. Sexual indulgence of any sort in a young man is a loss, not only to himself but also, prospectively, to that dear girl whom he will some day make his wife. Such reflections will often drive away the temptation entirely. If they are not sufficient to do so let him read some interesting book that shall take his mind away from the subject; or, that failing, let him take exercise, vigorous exercise—pushed to fatigue, if necessary. If these states of temptation occur in bed at night, let him rise and read, plunge his arm into very cold water, or if necessary go forth into the open air and seek relief in a rapid walk. It is better to go to any amount of trouble and to endure any physical discomfort, than to sacrifice one's chastity, the loss of which can never be replaced.

A young man naturally desires and expects chastity of the strictest order in the young woman of his choice for a wife. Who would marry a girl, no matter how beautiful or how many and varied her accomplishments if it were known that she had granted her favors to any other man? And yet, what less has *she* a perfect right to require from a young man who presumes to pay his addresses to her? This consideration, too, should serve as a restraint to any amorous desires that might infest a man's mind. It is wonderful how keen are the perceptions of a pure minded young lady to detect even an approach to licentiousness in the male. He is abhorrent to her and his very sphere betrays him.

With the facts of the preceding pages,

contained in this chapter being known, it does seem as if every man would keep himself pure from all carnal associations and use the utmost care not to prostitute his mind, that he may approach the nuptial altar as pure in mind and body as he would have her who is to become the idol of his heart.

Now this is all very beautiful in theory and desirable in practice, but *is it practical?* Can man so school himself in self denial as to accomplish this end? Are there not real physiological facts existing which utterly preclude the possibility of this most desirable result? Do not, as has been alleged by some writers, the testicles of man secrete semen until they become so surcharged that emission becomes absolutely necessary, and does not this accumulation actually produce such sexual excitement that man feels compelled to seek relief in some way? I answer, most unhesitatingly, NO! The above questions are all theories and utterly devoid of fact.

Would Almighty God command, "Thou shalt *not* commit adultery," and then so create man as to compel him to break his Divine injunction?

Abundance of proof is at hand to substantiate this sweeping remark of mine, were this the place to produce it. Seminal fluid is abundantly secreted and produced only during the heighth of sexual excitement in the male. As Acton remarks: "It is a highly organized fluid requiring the expenditure of much vital force in its elaboration and its expulsion." It is secreted from the blood of his body and the whole man physically, mentally and spiritually is concerned and represented in its product; consequently the action requires an effort of the whole man, and, if often repeated, the effect is very exhausting to the physical powers, to the mind and to the brain. Let this be another warning to remain in purity of heart.

We have said in the preceding pages that man, in a healthy state, need not lose a drop of seminal fluid until after marriage. There are many abnormal causes resulting in what are called wet dreams, nightly pollutions, spermatorrhœa, prostatic emission during stool or urination, also diurnal emissions without erection. These may result from over study, from errors in diet such as use of coffee, highly seasoned food, wines, spirituous liquors or drugs of various kinds—though perhaps prescribed by a physician. When these troubles arise from constitutional disorders, a skillful physician must be

*3

consulted at once. Errors in diet and the
taking of drugs causing this trouble must
of course be discontinued. * " Certain medi-
cines—as astringents, purgatives, narcotics,
stimulants and diuretics especially—may bring
on conditions from which spermatorrhœa may
arise." Among other causes Lallemand refers
to the use of quinine, tobacco and, particularly *alcohol.* The trouble may also arise
from injuries and many other accidental
causes, besides masturbation and venereal ex-
cesses.

It is distressing to see what a complete
wreck seminal losses make of those who
were once robust and healthy young men,
and what a shock they give to the nervous
system. They become weak, pale, and
feeble in mind, while all that was manly and
vigorous has gone out of them. Now which
of the two is preferable—the pride of a virtuous youth, or the roue' exhausted and worn
out by sexual abuses? It demands great
strength to become either, but really a much
greater effort for the latter; because it requires
very great perseverance for a chaste and pure
minded man to debase himself by such practices. It depends on the mind which is all
right before yielding the first point; therefore

---

* Lallemand and Wilson, page 192.

beware and shun the first step downward. Strengthen the moral courage and exercise the will power so as always to be able to say, " No," to whatever temptation the conscience tells you is wrong.

CHAPTER V.

Adolescence of the Female.

ADOLESCENCE of the female embraces the period of life from the age of twelve or fourteen, to twenty-one years.

At about the twelfth or fourteenth year of the girl's life a marked change comes over her form, features and mental state. Unlike the male, the forms which in him are angular, become in her rounded, symmetrical and beautiful, and the characteristic feminine proportions are well marked; she becomes more graceful in her movements, her voice grows sweeter, more mellow, more powerful and capable of registering a higher tone. New feelings and desires are awakened in her mind. Her deportment becomes more commanding and less frivolous, and the girl is lost in the woman.

If she has been so fortunate as to have escaped all the dangers and baneful influences of infantile and childhood life, she is womanly indeed, and we behold her with an unburdened conscience, clear intellect, artless and candid address, good memory, buoyant spirits, a

complexion bright, clear and, as the poet de-
clares, "beautiful exceedingly." Every function of her body is well performed, and no
fatigue is experienced after moderate exertion.
She evinces that elasticity of spirit and gracefulness of body, and happy control of her
feelings which indicate healthfulness of both
mind and body. Her whole time is given up
to her studies, duties and amusements; and
as she feels her stature increase and her intellect enlarge, she gladly prepares for her coming struggle with the world—though in a
manner becoming to her sex. This, too, is no
fanciful sketch, but is realized in thousands
of cases every year. It is one which parents
feel proud to witness in a daughter, and one
in which the daughter takes a modest delight.
We have said that every function of her body
is well performed. The functions of the female
body, which in a state of health are perfectly
free from pain, are very numerous and, in the
four years from fourteen to eighteen, she ac-
complishes an amount of physiological cell
change and growth which Nature does not
require of a boy in less than twice that num-
ber of years. It is obvious, therefore, that a
girl upon whom Nature, for a limited period
and for a definite purpose, imposes so great a
physiological task, will not have as much

power left for the tasks of school as a boy, of whom Nature requires less at the corresponding epoch. The functions of circulation, respiration, digestion, perspiration, nutrition and menstruation, though involuntary, are all important, dependent one upon another, and all develop at the proper time. Puberty is the proper time for the appearance of menstruation, one of the most important and sacred of her functions. It should not be feared, dreaded or regarded as a nuisance; it forms a part of herself; and she never commands the respect and forbearance of her friends, or even of her enemies, more than when it is known that she is "unwell." It serves in many ways as a blessing to her, rather than an inconvenience. Let no young girl be alarmed, as, owing to the negligence of her parents or guardians, many are, at the first appearance of this flow of blood from the genital organs. She should keep more quiet than usual, at these times, until the flow disappears, which it will do in a few days. In a state of health these appearances occur every twenty-eight days and the young lady should exercise extreme caution at such times, in avoiding unnecessary fatigue, exposure to cold, getting wet, suddenly cooling off when heated, etc. One of the reasons why so many suffer at this

time is due to the want of proper knowledge
and care, also for the want of a proper feeling
about the matter. I have known young ladies
to be guilty of the almost incredible crime of
trying to arrest the flow by plugging up the
vagina and by resorting to other means, that
they might attend a dancing party or some
pleasure excursion. Such a procedure is sure
to be followed by the direst retribution to the
offender. Nature never allows her laws to be
so trifled with. Some experience a deep
mortification on account of this function; some
think it a very great inconvenience and a
nuisance—an obstacle to their pleasure; others
feel unhappy and vexed about it. In truth,
every woman should consider it a privilege
and should regard menstruation as it really is,
a blessing from heaven; and, when rightly
performed, a help to lend loveliness to her
character, beauty to her expression, music to
her voice, and gracefulness to her form and
movements.

Mothers or guardians should instruct young
girls in good time as to the expected menstrual
function and prepare their minds for its advent.
They should also be carefully instructed in
regard to the external use of water—of its
attendant danger, lest they chill themselves
sufficiently to arrest this flow, which should

continue uninterruptedly until the function is complete. Too many lives have been sacrificed by suppressing the monthly flux; external ablutions should be plentiful, but only sufficient, as in the case of boys, for cleanliness. If menstruation should not become healthfully established at the proper time of age, consult a judicious physician who will see that any abnormal condition, preventing such consummation, is properly removed. " The principal organs of elimination, common to both sexes, are the bowels, kidneys, lungs and skin. A neglect of their functions is punished in each alike. To woman is intrusted the exclusive management of another process of elimination, viz.: the catamenial function. This, using the blood for its channel of operation, performs, like the blood, double duty. It is necessary to ovulation, and to the integrity of every part of the reproductive apparatus; it also serves as a means of elimination for the blood itself. A careless management of this function, at any period of life during its existence, is apt to be followed by consequences that may be serious; but a neglect of it during the epoch of development, that is, from the age of fourteen to eighteen or twenty, not only produces great evil at the time of the neglect, but leaves a large legacy of evil to the future.

The system is then peculiarly susceptible; and disturbances of the delicate mechanism we are considering, induced during the catamenial weeks of that critical age by constrained positions, muscular effort, brain work, and all forms of mental and physical excitement, germinate a host of ills." *

Here I must be allowed to protest most solemnly against the use of injections into the vagina for the so-called purpose of cleanliness. Vaginal syringes are constructed and used now by thousands and the sufferings of the human race are increased thereby ten thousand fold proportionately. The vagina, like all organs supplied with a mucous membrane, is self-cleansing. Water, or any other fluid thrown into this organ, has a tendency to disorder the mucous follicles, to dry up their secretions and thus prevent the efflux of some of Nature's necessities. From this cause alone there will be a reaction upon the vaginal walls, upon the neck of the uterus and the uterus itself; the ovaries also become disordered; the lungs sympathize as well as the throat and bronchial tubes, producing hoarseness, hacking cough and a host of troubles following in their train. Nervous headaches of fearful intensity are frequently produced

*Clarke: "Sex in Education."

from this unnatural course of procedure.
Moreover, water thrown into the vagina, to
wash it out, day after day for a considerable
time, absolutely produces a leucorrhœa most
persistent in character. This is the confession
of young ladies to me in making inquiry as
to the origin of their trouble, and I have
found that the discharge was unknown to
some of them till after the use of these injections. It stands to reason that such unnatural
washings should be followed by a retribution
equal to the error committed, because, as before stated, Nature's laws cannot be perverted
without a penalty. A girl should never, under
any pretext whatever, resort to such unhallowed
means for the cure or alleviation of leucorrhœa,
ulceration, or for any disorders that affect these
parts. By so doing she is really forming a
basis for innumerable future ills. If the girl
is well, she has none of these disorders, for
they all arise from constitutional derangements. As all must acknowledge, it is a
self-evident fact—that, *if a woman is well,
every part of her must be well also;* no one
organ can, unaided, get up a disease by itself.
In all troubles of this nature, as well as of any
other, consult a judicious physician.

There are objections, however, of even a
graver nature than those urged above against

the use of such instruments. They often
excite sensations in the parts to which they
are applied, that should remain perfectly dor-
mant in the unmarried state. After awhile
these sensations, increasing in frequency and
influence, serve to prostitute the mind and
the young lady may become ruined for life.
I am stating facts that can be proved by mul-
titudes of living witnesses to-day in cases
and confessions that have come under my
own observation. On remonstrating against
this habit, some remark, " But it feels so nice,
doctor!" Of course, ablutions of the *external*
organs are perfectly right and proper and should
be resorted to daily. To the reflecting mind no
more need be said about this matter. Those
who wish to live in harmony with the order
of their creation and thereby preserve the
freshness of health, will not have recourse to
such means as add new derangements to the
system.

To preserve feminine charms as the girl
develops into womanhood, much depends upon her mental state. She must not allow
herself to bear malice towards anyone, must
not plot evil or attempt to " pay off others in
their own coin," as it is called, or seek revenge
in any way; but she must ever cultivate a
forgiving disposition, good thoughts and good

feelings towards everyone. There is always danger of meeting both rude and lewd girls, and that too in places where least expected; they may be found in schools of all kinds and are occasionally met with in the houses of one's own friends. Not very long since a charming young lady wrote me from a neighboring city, that while sharing a bed with another girl, she experienced a very strange sensation induced by the improper liberties of her bed-fellow; and so persistent were these troublesome sensations, although occupying a bed by herself ever after, she thought it proper to seek my advice. Now this was a good and pure-minded girl who might easily have been ruined but for her inherent love of chastity; and so our daughters are always in danger of being contaminated. A perfectly pure and chaste mind, unsullied by impure thoughts or acts, and cultivated by the exercise of all the Christian virtues, lends enchantment to the eye, sweetness of expression to the face, music to the voice, and gracefulness of carriage. Cultivation of merely external manners will not do; they must spring from the mind and thence they shine throughout the whole, in every fibre and movement of the body. Such an one is truly beloved wherever she goes; she has a real affection for her father and mother, brothers and sisters; and she is fully prepared to appreciate and love one of the opposite sex whose purity of life and nobleness of mind fully corresponds to her own.

To retain this charm of excellence will cost her many a trial and her temptations will be innumerable and very great. But her perceptive faculties are keen, and at the first suspicion of anything wrong she must have the moral courage to say: "No! that is not allowable, it is not right," or, "this is impure and its tendency is to vice." Whatever the temptation may be, in thought or in deed, let no one persuade her into wrong-doing—not even her *apparently* best friend; for it would only be an appearance of friendship if he tempted to anything of a vicious nature. She will be beset with hosts of admirers, some of them pure and having honorable intentions; but (I am sorry to sound the note of warning here,) others will come with the most dishonorable intentions possible, though with an air of sincerity, and apparently as artless as doves. Study all men long and carefully, keeping them meanwhile at a respectful distance; never allow one to sit near with his arm about your waist or to hold your hand in his; never allow him to kiss you—*the vilest of loathsome diseases may be communicated by a kiss* viz.: *syphilis.* Do not allow any approach or touch beyond what is customary in the best of society at a social gathering. Many a young lady with an angelic form and spotless soul within, full of the best intentions and of the purest character, giving bright promise of a brilliant future, has been ruined for life by trusting herself alone with some of these apparently wise and good, yet really vile men.

Young women have not, as a rule, any sexual propensity, or amorous thoughts or feelings. If they have been properly educated and cared for, they are, before marriage, perfect strangers to any such sensations ; and yet any young lady who falls, does so by her own hand and she has no one else to blame for it. *Remember* that the Lord, in the beginning, never suffers temptations beyond one's strength to overcome. If she falls ultimately, it results from allowing an impure seed to be planted in the mind at first, which she then nourishes for a time and only in the end it bears its fruit.

As time passes, a young lady forms an acquaintance with gentlemen, and at length she favors the addresses of one who is particularly agreeable to her. After this acquaintance has ripened into love, and she has become convinced of the purity of his heart, she enjoys being with him, in sitting by his side, and is unhappy in his absence. When betrothed, owing to her great and pure love for him, she takes pleasure in receiving such marks of affection from him as are shown by a tender father or brother, but nothing more. After marriage, she feels that she is really his and that he has become a part of herself—that they are no more twain but are one flesh. All this has transpired without her hardly suspecting such a quality in herself as an amorous affection. Still she more than ever loves him, more than ever desires to be near him until finally their union is fully and truly consummated by the marriage act. At no time in her life does a woman make a greater sacrifice of her feelings than at this time, and she does it solely for her pure and fervent love for him. This is right and proper, and is in accordance with the laws of order in the creation of the two sexes in the human, animal and vegetable kingdoms throughout the world.

I wish here to have some "Plain Talk," that the true object of this book may be more fully understood and its mission more successfully accomplished. Unless willing to make the above sacrifice, no woman should ever marry; because she would not then be fulfil-

ling the marriage covenant. Besides, she
would be false to her husband and this falsity
might cause his moral and physical destruction ; his health would suffer and his
manhood become dethroned, because her
conduct would utterly controvert the immuta-
ble laws of nature. Nature's laws cannot
possibly be set aside without the infliction
of a severe penalty. The healthy young
woman will have no difficulty in preserving
her chastity intact, so long as she cultivates
that purity of mind to which she is naturally prone. She should never allow herself
to read immoral stories or books having in
the slightest degree even, such a tendency ;
theatrical plays with loose morals should
also be avoided, and light, silly novels are
very pernicious to the imaginative mind
of the young. On the other hand useful
reading stores the mind with high and
noble thoughts, whence spring good and useful deeds.

Unfortunately there are a variety of morbid
conditions to which the female is liable, so
that sexual desires arise in spite of every effort
to keep aloof from them—even though there
is not the slightest guilt in mental or bodily
transgression. These are owing to disordered
conditions of the sexual system, just as other

disorderly desires arise, and are often *inher-ited*—remember this all parents!—or they may be caused by some morbific influences, as are other diseased conditions of the body. Many a time have I had pure-minded young ladies apply to me for medical aid in these matters, confessing that they had impure thoughts which they knew were wrong, but of which they could not rid themselves. In such cases there are physical symptoms of some kind that incite these thoughts and feel-ings. The proper medical and hygienic treat-ment always restores order in such functional derangements and the sexual disturbances of the mind disappear. I have repeatedly cured nymphomania by curing physical, or consti-tutional symptoms. In one case which came under my care, nymphomania appeared in a married woman in the seventh month of her pregnancy, and so fearfully did her mania rage that it threw her into convulsions. Her physical and sensational symptoms led me to the choice of the medicine that cured her, so that she was happily delivered of a fine, healthy child at full term and no trace of the disease has ever appeared since. Too often young women err and give way to such feel-ings in resorting to *self-abuse* for relief, or to the caresses of the opposite sex, when they are ruined forever. It is never safe to temporize or to tamper in this way with such sensations. Women have heads and brains, as well as men, and rational faculties, too. Every digression allowed, only paves the way for others, with less and less resistance, and more and more ruinous results. Let a judicious physician be consulted at once in all cases where a morbid condition seems to excite immoral thoughts and sensations.

The effects of self-abuse upon woman, is as disastrous as masturbation upon males. A few hours after its commission, or the next day at furthest, she feels languid and dragged out, sleepy, unfit for reading· anything solid, or studying, and unfit for social enjoyment with others; she looks pale and haggard; often she feels giddy, particularly when rising in the morning, with many other discomforts too numerous to mention here. And is it true that some young ladies, the sweetest and fairest of our race, play with one another in an immodest and indecent way, teaching immorality to the pure and innocent? I fear it is, I *know* it is. Such things need not, must not, and will not be tolerated. This little book will go about in all classes of society confirming and strengthening the pure in heart in their purity and enlightening the

ignorant who will joyfully hail the good news;
all will join hands in one popular cry against
indecencies and indulgences of an impure
nature; and the vilest man even will be taught
to fear and respect the combined world of
chaste female influence.   So it must be and
eventually will be;   but woman, naturally
pure and lovely woman! the greatest part of
this work must be done by you.

CHAPTER VI.

MARRIAGE.

The Husband.

" AND JEHOVAH GOD said, It is not good that the man should be alone; I will make him a help meet for him. * * * * And JEHOVAH GOD brought the woman unto the man. And the man said, This is now bone of my bones and flesh of my flesh. Therefore shall a man leave his father and his mother, and shall cleave unto his wife: and they shall be one flesh."—Gen. ii. 18, 22-24.

"The marriage of one man with one woman is therefore designed in our very creation by Him who made us. The love which brings them together and binds them together, flows into their minds from the Divine Love, from the love which has operated hitherto, and which now operates, in creating and forming a Heaven of human beings."

All young men, on arriving at the age of twenty-five, other circumstances being favorable, should conform to the laws of Divine order and marry. "Whom shall we marry?

Young ladies now-a-days require such an outfit and it costs so much to support a wife in the style she wishes to live, or has been accustomed to, that, to say nothing of the extra expense of children, we cannot afford to marry." This is a wrong view to take, because, pomp, style and show *are not the true objects of marriage!* The married state is a duty and a great privilege, while its uses are of the highest possible order physically, mentally and spiritually. The love which brings the two together and which should bind them together, requires only a comfortable home of respectable appearance. Young married people should begin like young married people; it is more orderly and more conducive to the welfare and true happiness of each that, as time passes on, they build up their fortunes together, each helping the other—thus affording new charms that no other course will or can yield.

In the choice of a wife, a man should especially seek *congeniality.* He should make the acquaintance of a young lady living and moving in the same sphere of life as his own, such as is congenial to his tastes; he should see her in company with other young people and observe how she treats them; and particularly notice how she acts towards her

father and mother, brothers and sisters : for a
good daughter and sister always makes a
good wife. Study closely her character, her
mental discipline, her tastes in reading and
her mode of life generally. Above all, note
her disposition as to selfishness, whether she
be determined and bent upon having her own
way in everything, or whether she is yielding
and thoughtful of the comfort and happiness
of her associates. Remember that in the
married state there must be a mutual yielding
to each other, though not the sinking of the
wife's identity, so that the combined life of the
two may become one harmonious whole.
Observe what she thinks of children and get
her opinion as to how they should be brought
up and educated. Be sure that she is one
who can be loved most tenderly, one for
whom a man can make any sacrifice in reason
for her sake—for whom one can deny himself
any comfort, any and every passion, brave any
danger, and conquer every difficulty in his
power, to make her life happy and useful.
One quality : Is she strictly virtuous ? Is she
chastity itself in thought, word and deed?
If you, young man, have been the same,
if you have held yourself in by "bit and bridle,"
as it were,—then, if she reciprocates your love,
you are at liberty to propose marriage to her.

Before marriage, a young man takes great pains to make himself attractive, is very attentive and polite, keeps up a genteel appearance and is civility itself, that he may woo and win the young lady most nearly approaching his ideal of feminine perfection, and the one most nearly suited to his tastes and congeniality. After marriage he feels that she is his, that she has pledged herself to this effect; and the law has so decided; she is his, as he is hers, irrevocably. Now, young man, do you mean to be loyal, to be her real husband until death dissolves the allegiance? Then let nothing cool your ardor. Be as watchful as when you were her wooer and even more so. Let nothing induce you to swerve from your duty, to violate your vow or to betray your trust. But ever be faithful and true. So may you be accounted worthy of her choice as a husband and worthy to be enrolled among the respected and honored fathers in our land. Heavier responsibilities rest upon you now than before marriage. Your wife must be protected, supported and cared for in every possible way, and you need to be even more careful to retain her love than you were to win it. You are under heavy responsibilities to your relatives and the community in which you live, that your

united lives bear such fruit as will be to all a
delight. Together, in your unity, you form
as it were a tree ; your united lives throw
out branches and leaves, buds and blossoms,
and finally fruit in its season ; and every tree
is known by its fruit. Bearing in mind the
high duties to which as a husband and a
father you are called, seek not to live for carnal pleasures. You have struggled manfully
with yourself and the world and have come
up to this stage of your life pure and uncon-
taminated ; and that love which brought you
two together, now flows into your united lives
from the Divine Love. Let that love continually operate through you unitedly in creating
new human beings who shall ultimately serve
to swell the grand army of the Angelic hosts
in Heaven.

Some well-meaning and otherwise appar-
rently good husbands, but not true, form
habits of staying from their homes during
their leisure hours, particularly in the even-
ings. They visit club houses, billiard rooms
or other places of amusement, leaving their
wives at home. Such absences distress a
wife greatly, though her love often restrains
any expression of disapproval. These habits
increase, she suffers more and more, loses
sleep on his account and her health fails. The

husband's dissipations grow upon him—all such desertions are dissipations when they become habitual—until he loses all relish for the company of his faithful wife and for the caresses of his young and lovely children, until finally to stay at home a single evening is a restraint and unhappiness to him. Where now is the plighted faith! Where now is the tree, its branches and leaves with their buds and blossoms, and what is the fruit? Where now is that pure love which he promised when they became united and which should forever bind them together, and who has almost severed that love? Has not the little that remains become merely carnal, on his part at least? Where is that union of mind and communion of soul that lifts one above sensualism; and without which, sensualism is the only link and quality left to keep the two together, until death dissolves the union?

CHAPTER VII.

MARRIAGE [CONTINUED].

The Wife.

YOUNG ladies why do you marry? Through infancy, childhood and adolescence you have been watched over most tenderly and cared for most lovingly; you have been protected and educated, and have been made as happy under the paternal roof as circumstances would allow; and this very book has been written largely on *your* account. It has been the custom from time immemorial, as it always will be, for girls to complete their education and then to marry. But alas! how very few seem to realize what married life really is and what will be expected in it; what its duties and responsibilities are, or even what leads to marriage. But to the question why do you even think of getting married? The answer is, "Because it is inherent in the mind of every true female character. It was ordained of God in her creation, spiritually, mentally, and physically—from her inmost being to her complete ultimation. It was in the very design of her creation that she should love and be loved, that she should be sought after by the male sex, and that she should become a wife and mother."

First, let us understand what "marriage" signifies. The word itself has the same meaning as the Latin word *conjugium* and represents a conjunction or union together. Carried out to its higher or more interior meaning, marriage signifies the joining of good and truth—the "good" being represented by the woman and "truth" being represented by the man. Hence it denotes the spiritual conjunction of minds, and thence of bodies, in contradistinction to the merely natural conjunction or joining together of bodies only. So, to secure a real marriage, there must be a spiritual conjunction of minds; and the conjunction of bodies in wedlock is simply the ultimation, or manifestation of spiritual principles in marriage.

The true reason why girls marry is because they have an innate principle of love for the male sex; and this love is drawn from the Lord above. Consequently, it is pure, chaste, and when fully developed, very powerful. In connection with this principle comes the desire to be sought after and loved by a man of congenial character for whose dear sake a woman is induced to leave father and mother, brothers and sisters, to become the wife of him whom she can claim as her own dear husband. This Heaven-born principle is what leads and induces the female to assent to the marriage relation. For her own sake, for his sake as well as for the sake of all parties concerned, this step should be taken very carefully and only after mature consideration. Once married, there is no escape from its life-long duties and responsibilities. She must yield to him whatever the marriage vow allows, that she may become a *wife* in the fullest sense of the term. Marriage is a sacred relation, instituted by God Himself, and the sexual approach which follows between husband and wife, is a special avowal of their relation to each other; and so often as it is repeated it is a renewal of their obligations to be faithful to each other. All sexuality is in the order of creation and, coming from the Lord, serves for high and holy purposes. It was *never* intended for mere carnal pleasure; as such, it is the profanation and perversion of a great boon to the human race. The man or woman who perverts it must and will, sooner or later, suffer a penalty equal to the transgression.

The husband rightfully expects to find in his wife, as a seal of the marriage covenant,

his greatest possible delight. It should be
her greatest delight to give him that pleasure;
and if she loves her husband according to her
avowal, she will not fail to do this. The feeling, each of the other's nearness—in thought,
word and act, as though each one were inter-
twined with the other in the most complete
union, is a very great delight; even indescrib-
ably great. The sexual act itself is really a
type of the perfect harmony in which the
married pair should dwell throughout their
lives. It teaches a mutual yielding so that
the honeymoon, rising so beautifully and lovingly, may continue to wax lighter and brighter
and its fullness be attained in this world only
at the dissolution, by a natural death, of a
union so orderly and happily formed. It
is in the very nature of the male to seek
his mate; it is an inborn principle for him to
do so, and his health, even his life, certainly
his moral life, often depends upon an orderly
and lawful indulgence of what this inherent
principle demands. The greatest longevity
and the best health are found among fathers
and mothers; thereby proving that orderly
and well-regulated sexual intercourse is just
as necessary to the married couple as are the
functional demands of all other organs of the
body. From the foregoing it may be plainly

inferred, that, if the wife of a chaste young
man who has duly guarded himself from
his childhood up, until he has sought and
wedded his mate, fails to reciprocate cheer-
fully and pleasantly in the seal of connubial
affection, she proves a bitter disappointment
to him. Not that he is carnal, gross or beastly,
no! The principle given him by his Creator
and residing in his pure and inmost soul has
been violated by her in whom he placed his
life's confidence; she has proved *false* to
him in this particular, one upon which their
present and eternal welfare so largely depends.
Young ladies about to marry should be taught
to understand this matter most fully, in all
its bearings. If they pervert marriage in
false practices, the love of God, conjugal love,
and the love of infants, the three holiest and
noblest inspirations of life, perish together. No
woman then should ever marry without a full
knowledge of her duties to her husband, particularly in the sexual respect; for without
granting this privilege to her husband in full
and free accord, there *cannot* be maintained
a happy married life.

The duties of marriage, as a topic, embrace
a vast field of thought; and there is *so much*
to say thereon, so much advice to tender, so
many absolute commands to enjoin, so many

warnings to utter, that it is with difficulty I restrain myself from launching out diffusely in an attempt to give the most important of these. But to so specifically particularize is not the purpose of this book. Enough is said herein, I trust, to set the reflective mind to thinking seriously on these matters and thereby to awaken the conscience to a full sense of its duties. Quite too many cases have come under my observation where the marriage vow has never been consummated or, if consummated at all, in a very begrudging manner, owing to the insubordination of the wife. Consequently dissatisfaction, unhappiness and frequently a permanent separation follows, bringing disgrace upon the family and scandal to their circle of friends. This is not only wrong, but it is a most unpardonable vice. Sexuality has been ordained by God in his wisdom as the means of creation. It exists throughout all nature, in every tree, plant and shrub, in every animal and insect; in every bird that flies, in every fish that swims, in every man and woman. The very best and purest of husbands and wives, all the world over, indulge in sexuality to their united satisfaction, in full acknowledgment that it is of God and from God. Every wife who is unreasonable or derelict in this *duty* is untrue to her hus-

band and commits a sin against the God of
Heaven and earth. Since, then, sexuality is
so evidently of Divine appointment, it should
be committed entirely to him in its effects.*

If at any time the act prove fruitful and a
child be born, it should be considered as a
great blessing and gift from God Himself.
What is more beautiful than to see a married
couple engaged in rearing a new human being destined to become an angel in Heaven!
For this indeed is the prime object of sexuality
and of the marriage covenant. As has been
well said, life on earth is Heaven's seminary.
And yet, so many wives, to their shame be it
said, use preventives to conception, thus at-
tempting to controvert the order of Nature
and Nature's God; this is one of the greatest
crimes of the present age and vengeance will
surely be taken on every transgressor in this
sacred matter. Such practice is secret vice
which little by little wears upon the inmost
vital principle until the perpetrators of such
wrongs suffer untold misery in their physical
nature—often not even suspecting the cause
of such sufferings.

"But there is yet another reason, and a
very strong moral one, why the wife should
not remain childless. There can be no ques-

---

*See "In Health." By Dr. A. J. Ingersoll, Corning, N. Y.

tion that the blood of the father mingles with that of the mother through the medium of the child *in utero.* (Hence the transmission of blood-diseases from husband to wife.) Hence the indelible impressions made upon a wife by the father of her offspring—impressions, both mental and physical, which by character or resemblance she often transmits to her children by a second husband.* Now, * * * * may not this account for the similarity of character and identity of tastes, and, indeed, for that wonderful personal resemblance, which sometimes develops between husband and wife? And does not this requisite alone fulfil the Divine interpretation of marriage, that 'they are no more twain but one flesh?'"*

After marriage a new order of life is entered upon by the wife, and her family matters should subordinate all other schemes and projects of her future existence. Her main thought and study should now be, "How can I best fulfil these new duties and responsibilities? First, my dear husband! how can I be a true help-meet to him? Here we two are to be one, a new *punctum saliens,* and every act of ours will bear the image of our united lives. No matter what may happen, I will be

* Wm. Goodell, M. D., "Lessons in Gynecology," P. 442.
4*

true to my matrimonial vow and to my God;
for I am in His hands and my dear husband's." A married life begun in this way,
with such resolutions sincerely and studiously
kept, will secure a life full of happiness and
privileges beyond the fondest hope and ex-
pectation. When pregnancy occurs, just as
soon as the fact be suspected, the little embryo
should be regarded as already a member of
the family. Every act of each parent should
now be performed in some degree with
reference to the forth-coming infant. The
mother's thoughts particularly should be di-
rected to it as much as possible whilst per-
forming the uses of life. She should read
much that is elevating and ennobling in character as this serves a good purpose in producing a more perfect, more healthy and more
brilliant child. Let her read such books as
" Elements of Character " by Miss Chandler;
" Growth of the Mind " by S. Reed; " Sex in
Education " by E. H. Clarke, M. D.; also,
" Wear and Tear " by S. Weir Mitchell, M. D.;
and any other books of like character. Do
not forget that the education of the child begins *in utero*.

During gestation the mother should subsist
as far as possible upon fruit, vegetables and a
farinaceous diet—always plain and without

spices. Plenty of active exercise is indispensable and the use of a " Health Lift " will be
found most beneficial. When the nine months
are completed, under care of a competent
physician, the birth of the child will be accomplished with but comparatively little pain, and
its attendant dangers and difficulties will be
greatly lessened.

CHAPTER VIII.

MARRIAGE [CONCLUDED].

Husband and Wife.

TO preserve the marriage vow inviolate,
the same pure love that brought the
two together should be cultivated by
home uses and home amusements such as
readings, games, conversation, etc. If the
wife have needle work, let the husband read
or talk to her; if he be a literary man, let her
presence cheer him on and inspire him to
nobler and more refined productions. What
was done during courtship that made time
pass so rapidly and so pleasantly? Was
every topic so discussed and used up that
nothing is now left for an exchange of views?
Is carnal pleasure to be the only binding tie?
Such a life is not very pure and only a poor
use can be made of it. Topics of interest to
a married pair should be innumerable and
their pleasures inexhaustible. Home is the
soil in which the tree is to grow; and the
richer the soil, the better for the tree, and the
more numerous will be the branches, all of
them vigorously developing buds and leaves,

blossoms and fruit, which will be most fragrant, beautiful and useful. When amusement outside of home is sought let it be, as far as possible, of a nature that both may enjoy it equally.

Husband and Wife! He, being of larger mould in every particular, in head, chest, and all the vital organs, is the provider, the protector, the guardian of his home; he, the masculine, or representative of the Truth, is to lead the way in conducting home or business affairs. She, the feminine, or representative of the Good, inclines to the good way continually; and, as married partners, Good and Truth should be married in them. There cannot be a true evil way nor a good false way; there can only be a true good way and a good true way. So the wife, the good, must conjoin herself to her husband, the truth, in order that every truth may result in good; and the husband, the truth, should seek to be conjoined to the wife, the good, that every good may become true. In this there is much wisdom: if the husband be truly wise he will always be sure that all his projects are tempered with good; while if the wife be truly good, all her doings will be enlightened by truth. As hand in hand they thus go through life's planning and doing, the husband will always be assisted by his good, the wife; and the wife will be led on in good by her truth, the husband. By taking this high and holy ground, there will be experienced pleasure and happiness by the married couple, far transcending all other modes of life in existence. Then will each and every organ in the body be seen to have a fitness, a place, and a use which could not possibly be dispensed with, because, each and all these organs have an originating cause in the mental and spiritual parts of mankind, from which they proceed and from which they exist. Thus we see how wrong, how frightfully wrong it is to abuse, or pervert the use of, *any* of these physical organs which are so sacred and so important to the welfare of the human family. "Dishonor the body, the temple of the soul, and you dishonor the soul." "If any man defile the temple of God, him will God destroy."—I. Cor. 3:17.

When married, the battle for one united and harmonious life really begins. The wife's great and supreme love for her husband personally, will allow many privileges which under other circumstances her timidity and chastity would refuse. Tenderly and with great consideration should these privileges be accepted. For, contrary to the opinion of many men, there is no sexual passion on the part of the bride that induces her to grant such liberties. Then how exquisitely gentle and how forbearing should be the bridegroom's deportment on such occasions! Sometimes such a shock is administered to her sensibilities that she does not recover from it for years; and in consequence of this shock, rudely or thoughtlessly administered, she forms a deeply rooted antipathy against the very act which is the bond and seal of a truly happy married life. These sexual unions serve to bring the married pair into a perfectly harmonious relation to each other. And just as tenderly, lovingly and harmoniously should they join in each and all the daily uses of life which they are called upon to perform. The sexual relation is among the most important uses of married life; it vivifies the affections for each other, as nothing else in this world can, and is a powerful reminder of their mutual obligations to one another and to the community in which they live. Indulgence, however, should not be too frequent, lest it debilitate the pair and undermine their health. The bridegroom and husband should carefully watch over his bride and wife to see that she is not a sufferer and should govern himself accordingly. It is better that these renewed obligations should be made at stated periods, as man is governed so much by habit. As a rule, once or twice a week, or in some cases once in two weeks, is sufficient; but once a week will suffice in many cases for healthful purposes. During the menstrual flow there should be an entire cessation of the conjugal act. When pregnancy occurs it is in most cases, more healthful and better for the expectant mother to allow intercourse at regular times, very gently, throughout her gestation.

The object of marriage is the ultimation of that love which brings the two together and binds them together, in the procreation and rearing of children for Heaven. This is the only true aim and sole object about which every earthly desire, interest and plan of the married pair should cluster.

As to the question of child-bearing. No greater crime in the sight of Heaven exists to-day than that of perverting the natural uses of marriage. This is done in a great variety of ways, every one of which is criminal, in whatever form practised; and none will escape the penalty—no, not one. Nature's laws are inexorable; every transgression thereof is surely punished, even at the *climacteric period*, if not before. The questions of failing health, of physical inability, or too frequent conceptions are matters for the investigation, advice and decision of an experienced, judicious and upright physician. They should never be taken in hand and judged upon by the parties themselves. And to the objection "can't afford to have children; they cost too much," I have faith enough to reply, "Our Heavenly Father never sends more mouths than he can feed." Let each one do his and her duty in life and this cavil falls to the ground like water—which, when spilled, cannot be gathered up.

Good people everywhere rejoice when they behold a married couple living together in an orderly manner and rearing a large family of children. How often is Queen Victoria held up as a pattern of excellence in this respect: she accepted and acknowledged Prince Albert as her husband and gave herself to him as his wife; and so indeed she was in every sense of the term. Although a Queen, sitting on the pinnacle of power, she did not seek to avoid the pangs, the dangers or inconveniences of child-bearing. By her own personal strength her twelve children were brought forth and her own sensitive fibres and tissues felt the suffering. She nursed, caressed and loved them like a good mother and she was a *royal mother!* Other kings and queens

have done likewise; other husbands and
wives, high in power, wealth and fashion have
done and are still doing the same. And how
much the less should we, in the humbler walks
of life, obey the Divine command "Be fruitful and multiply."

If a husband truly loves his wife and if she
truly loves him, they will live for each other
and in each other, and they will be one; and
they will seek to do right in every particular
of their marital relation. To apply to life
the truths advanced above and to realize
them, will require great effort by the parties
in question. This manner of life will not
come of itself; it is too good to come
without working for. Mutual concessions
must be made daily, and several times a
day; one's own way must frequently be
given up, and always when discovered to be
a selfish way, because the mutual good is always to be consulted. Questions of importance should be discussed freely and dispas-
sionately, and a good reason be established
before adopting actions that may not lead to
proper results. In the marriage co-partner-
ship the interest in the right and the wrong, the
loss and the gain, the lights and the shadows,
the pleasures and the pains, should be equally
shared; because they concern one just as

much as the other, and should be equally
enjoyed, and equally borne by both.

A start is made with loving hearts and this
state of affairs must never be allowed to di-
minish. The husband should ever be glad
to see his wife, and the wife should ever be
glad to see her husband. How many husbands never know what reception they will
meet with on returning home after their anxious and exhausting business hours are over
for the day; it may be a happy or a very
unhappy one. How much it consoles, en-
courages, lifts up, and rests a man to return
to his home after the trying scenes of a day
busily spent in providing for the support of
his family are over, to find his wife affectionate and serene, and all about the house brilliant with contentment. Such a wife if she
has troubles, and of course she has just as
many troubles as the husband, though of a
different kind, and wishes to call the attention
of her husband to them, will do it at a proper
time, when she knows it will annoy him the
least, and when he will be able to give her the
most assistance. She will never try to annoy
him; but endeavoring to be a true help-meet
will seek in a proper and loving way to get
him to be the same to her. The wife will
gain and command the respect of her

husband only through kind and loving ways. By her love constantly and judiciously administered she will lead him onward and upward to higher aspirations and better circumstances in life, throughout their days of united existence. A scolding, fretting, worrying and selfish wife has ruined for life many a husband.

All the "self-denial" however, as it is called by some, is not on the wife's side; the husband too must be forbearing; he must remember on his way home at night that his faithful wife, who has been at home all day, has had trials and disappointments in her domestic affairs; and he must not be disappointed to find domestic arrangements a little disordered, and his wife somewhat chagrined that, under the circumstances, she really could give him no better a reception than he may experience. He must always try to make the best of it and be satisfied. He must not find fault with the cooking, for instance, but must be perfectly content with everything as it is until his well-managing wife has had time to overcome her difficulties and troubles.

Never find fault with your wife under any circumstances; let your intellect discover a way to better things if need be. A really wise man will never allow a harsh word to escape his lips to a loving wife, or to his harmless children. By so living together a wise husband and a loving wife will soon discover that they two are but complemental to each other—like the Will and Understanding of one individual.

CHAPTER IX.

TO THE UNFORTUNATE.

LET no one imagine that, because he or she has committed any of the great errors enumerated in former chapters, there is no hopeful future. Such a conclusion need not, necessarily, be accepted. In very many cases where there is a *will* to reform, there is also a *way*; and very often a complete cure and restoration to health may be effected. Diseased bones may be made sound; ulcerations healed; sore throats cured; blemishes on the skin removed; urinary difficulties may be dissipated or at least greatly ameliorated; sexual disorders remedied; impaired eyes much improved and defective vision much benefited if not wholly restored; the auditory apparatus helped if not fully cured; and the distracted mind, with its fanciful imageries, rendered tranquil and rational.

To accomplish all this the *mind* must lead the way. The brain must assert its supremacy, and the will-power become absolute. It is only where there is a will, an indomitable will, that a way out of these direful difficulties

is afforded. Let happen what may, no
opposing influences should dampen the determination to press forward to reformation;
and then, sooner or later, the conquest will
be made.

To begin with, when the mind is fully determined to overcome all obstacles or perish in
the attempt, consult a judicious physician as
advised in the preface of this book. Lose
no time with quackery in any shape or form.
Do not be beguiled by those who promise "a
speedy cure." Speedy cures cannot be made
in these cases. Strong determination to
improve aided by proper medication can, in
bad cases, only restore a healthful condition
in from two to three years. The system
requires to be made over anew as it were.
The current of life must be turned into new
channels. New thoughts and new blood must
be made to take the place of what were
wrong and polluted. This will take time
and perseverance; and then, little by little
the old enemies will be overcome and driven
out. But progress for the better must be
measured only from month to month and
even then there may be apparent relapses.
Let me however asseverate, from my abundance of experience in these cases, that there
is ultimately, after a reasonable time, every

hope of becoming sound and healthy again.

Many young persons are rendered quite distracted by the sexual instinct being too strong. It infests them and goads them on to the commission of further unseemly acts— though suffering much from past transgressions —which it seems almost impossible to avoid. The sensation haunts and clings to them day and night, in spite of every attempt to rise superior thereto. Sometimes nocturnal pollutions, or "wet dreams," as they are commonly termed, result from these or other causes. There must be some cause for this state of things and a rigid examination into one's mode of life should ascertain the same. It may come from errors in diet, in eating or drinking; in the use of highly seasoned food; or the taking of some medicinal drug substance. It is well known that many drugs have the power of producing such a condition. Should any of the above seem to act as causes, a change should be made at once. The plainest diet and simplest mode of life is always best in sickness or in health. Again, one may take too little exercise in the open air. If so, an abundance of physical exertion should be made daily, to insure a natural and healthy condition of all organs of the body. Or, uncomfortable conditions may arise, as they often

do, from some morbid condition of the
vital forces. If diet and exercise are in-
sufficient, the judicious physician should be
consulted and every symptom or unnatural
sensation from the crown of the head to the
soles of the feet, should be carefully described
to him. In all probability he will remedy the
trouble, thus restoring peace and happiness.
The generative organs are as liable to be
affected by a morbid state of the vital forces,
as are any other organs of the body; and
when so affected they are just as amenable to
treatment.

The above condition of affairs is not, however, confined to the male sex. Females
often suffer equally and in the same way.
Many young persons, of both sexes, have
fallen victims to these disorders who could
have been cured by proper medical treatment.
A female suffering from the ill effects of any
bad habit contracted in youth, or from any
sexual or venereal disorder, should seek
medical aid with the same promptness and
openness of heart as a male. To overcome
the vicious habit of self-abuse is no trifling
matter; it will require the persistent application of indomitable will, aided by Christi-
anity—by oft repeated appeals to the Lord
for aid, who lends a willing ear and

a helping hand to the poor and needy. When reformation is determined upon, it is better to consult a physician at once and act under his advice. Besides directing the proper diet and plenty of vigorous exercise in the open air, he will prescribe the proper medicament.

Cases of real syphilitic poisoning are most serious affections, and everyone should know of the fearful effects of this poison—how searchingly it infests the whole system, and how it contaminates the blood and every tissue in the body. Such cases, therefore, should not be trifled with in any way. Advertised nostrums should be particularly avoided. For, if this poison be simply smothered in one's blood instead of being wholly eradicated and cured, it will be sure to seize upon the offspring and either destroy them before birth or during dentition. The bare fear of such contamination should be amply sufficient to deter everyone from exposing him—or herself, to the risk. But, having fallen, by all means seek the aid of a judicious physician. An experience of nearly forty years in the treatment of these cases, in both sexes, has given me the power to know whereof I speak; and I do declare that a very large percentage of these cases can be cured in a safe manner; and so perfectly cured too, that there will be no danger of transmitting the infection to the offspring. I, by no means stand alone in this statement; many other physicians, after long years of experience assert the same truth.

Therefore, let no one be discouraged, no matter how far he, or she, has strayed from the paths of virtue or how much suffering has been entailed thereby. In connection with the physician's help, aid yourself. Have courage! Let the invincible will lead on unflinchingly—upheld by pure thoughts, and good actions will surely follow. "Desire is really dangerous only when it brings voluptuous pictures incessantly before the imagination. It thus holds a thousand conflicts with virtue which it conquers in the end; it installs itself in the bosom of the intelligence of which it becomes the habitual pre-occupation." Seek therefore for only pure thoughts.

We should at all times exert all the power within us to live correct and blameless lives in every respect, but particularly so in sexual matters. The happiness, the health, and the lives of families and communities are far more largely dependent upon these matters than is commonly supposed. Those who

have led lives of blameless ·purity, will
continue to do so after reading this book;
while those who have gone astray will here
find every encouragement to set about their
reformation at once. If faithful to the teachings recorded in these pages they will bless
the day and the occasion that inspired the
writer to put his hand to this work. The
God of Heaven and Earth knows that the
motive that led me to this undertaking
was pure, and as solely for the good of
humanity, as that purity which prompts a
human being to live a blameless life in the
sight of his Maker.

CHAPTER X.

From Whence does the Sex Proceed and What Determines It?

SO much has been written about this matter, and so many foolish, low, and really debasing theories and speculations have been advanced in relation thereto, that I deem it expedient at this time, and in this place, to put forth the true theory of the reproduction of the sexes, one that can endure the test of the most rigid scientific investigation. The only theory upon this subject worthy of notice, must be based upon a principle that will hold good and true throughout all animated nature, not only in the animal, but in the vegetable kingdom as well.

The earth is the common mother of the vegetable world; seeds of all kinds fall into her and she brings forth male and female plants according to the seeds planted. The *earth* certainly does not give the sex to plants for they come forth according to the life inherent in the seed; if this life-force be male, the plant must be male; and if the life-force

117

of the seed be female, the product must be a female plant. The earth can possibly bring forth no other sex than that which the life-force of the seed impels.

This is true in the animal creation. Within the female grows the seed given her by the male, be it male or female, and she can grow none other. In other words the male as is very evident on mature reflection gives the soul or the inmost vital principle, and the female clothes that soul, or gives it a body in which to operate. What else can the male do; what office does he perform, if it is not strictly this: to impart of his life-giving spirit! The mother in clothing this germ of life commingles, intertwines, and insinuates her own spirit, at the same time educating, instructing, and determining its development according to the influence she imparts to it. So the offspring partakes largely of the nature of both its parents. The determination as to whether he begets a male or female depends entirely upon the inmost vital state of the male at the time of giving, although he is unconscious of the fact, so that he can have no choice and no regulation, as some writers most absurdly claim, in the matter of the forth-coming sex. He determines or produces it unconsciously and involuntarily, the mother simply receiving, clothing, and issuing from her body what the father has given-her.

It must not be forgotten when exploring these deep subjects that man is a spiritual being, clothed with a material body, that his spirit is his inmost, and that what proceeds from him in the generative act has life from his inmost; consequently the life-giving principle of his semen is from his inmost, which constitutes its life-giving power. This inmost from the male, the begetting power, is clothed by his seminal fluid for an Allwise purpose; it is not the gross material, the clothing, that begets, but the living power which this material contains, which fructifies, or becomes conjoined, or commingled with the vital force of the ovule of the mother,* so that she can clothe it; and when so conjoined the germ, or seed, is planted in congenial soil. Conception has thus really taken place by virtue of this act, and the animal mother proceeds with her reproduction precisely upon the same general principles that mother earth reproduces corn from a single kernel.

It is universally acknowledged that the Lord creates, that we owe all to Him, that He gives us our children, etc., etc. This is true,

---

* See Guernsey's Obstetrics, 3d edition, on Reproduction.

and it is also true that He makes use of the
parents, through whom he operates to this end.
By the constant influx of his Divine Love
and Wisdom He gives us life, and by virtue
of this constant influx into the father who
begets, the mother's conception becomes
doubly sacred. She conceives from her
husband, and at the same instant the Lord
by virtue of His Divine Power breathes into
that conception the breath of life, whereby it
becomes a living soul. By the light of this
truth we see that it is not the parents who
give life to their offspring. They only supply
the pure material substances which are organized into the human form by the living and
life-giving forces which constantly flow in
from the Lord who is life itself and from whom
all life constantly emanates.

INDEX.

121